THE FRIENDSHIP OF WOMEN

THE FRIENDSHIP OF WOMEN

The Hidden Tradition
of the Bible

JOAN CHITTISTER

BlueBridge

 Benetvision

Cover design by Cynthia Dunne
Cover image by Art Resource, New York
Text design by Cynthia Dunne

The Scripture references are from the New Revised Standard Version
Bible: Catholic Edition © 1993 and 1989 by the Division of Christian
Education of the National Council of the Churches of Christ in the
U.S.A. Used by permission. All rights reserved.

Library of Congress Cataloging-in-Publication Data
Chittister, Joan.
The friendship of women : the hidden tradition of the Bible /
Joan Chittister.
p. cm.
ISBN 1-933346-02-7
1. Women in the Bible. 2. Female friendship—Biblical teaching.
3. Friendship—Religious aspects—Christianity. I. Title.
BS575.C5345 2006
241'.6762082—dc22
2005035246

Published by
B l u e B r i d g e
An imprint of
United Tribes Media Inc.
240 West 35 Street, Suite 500
New York, NY 10001
www.bluebridgebooks.com
Printed in the United States of America
10 9 8 7 6

CONTENTS

It takes a lot of friends
to write a book about friendship.
I am grateful to all of them.

INTRODUCTION

Friendship colors the very air we breathe. It is everywhere around us. We can see it in the eyes of old women in the kitchens of the women they love. We can hear it in the voices of one young woman giggling to another over the phone. We can feel it beating in our own hearts on lonely rainy days in faraway places when, most alone, we are haunted by the memory of those who have walked through life with us, and walk with us still. Friendship binds past and present and makes bearable the uncertainty of the future.

But friendship is, at best, an elusive concept, a movable feast. The word itself shifts in meaning from historical period to historical period. The understanding of it shifts from person to person, from relationship to relationship. The category splits and shades and nuances almost into oblivion at times. Friendship, we know, is sometimes "best" and sometimes "good." It is often "casual" and commonly "occasional." It ranges from the mellow to the saturating. It is no single thing ever, and yet there is no doubt of what it is when we have it.

The question of the place and nature and value of friendship has been, over the centuries, the fascination of philosophers, the quandary of scholars, the invisible sacrament of spiritual teachers, and the grail of mystics, artists, and poets. Whatever the context out of which the discussion springs, friendship is, in the end, always and everywhere eternal mystery, eternal desire. It is a grasp at the ultimate, the quest for human understanding.

"Two are better than one," the Book of Ecclesiastes teaches, "for if they fall, the one will lift the other up; but woe to the one that is alone. . . ." It's a simple statement, a profound one, this biblical commonplace. But the conventional wisdom of a highly mobile, basically anonymous, totally fragmented society affects, at the least, to ignore it. "No one is indispensable," we say so flippantly, so unfeelingly in a massified culture. But these words grate like sandpaper on the soul of the wizened and the loving. The sophisticates who say them are able, in this whirl of isolates, to pawn themselves off as wise and humble, even holy, for the claiming of them. The fact is, though, that the saying is woefully, pitiably, glaringly wrong. In the face of Ecclesiastes it simply shrivels away in the hold of a more searing and truer truth.

There is indeed one thing that renders all of us, any of us, indispensable. As long as there is someone, somewhere whose life breathes in time with my own, I know down deep that I am indeed needed, that I have no right to die. I know that I am truly indispensable, irreplaceable, vital to a life beyond my own. To that person I *am* indispensable. Whatever my own needs, the love of the other has greater claim on me than I do on myself. Our friends depend on us. Cicero wrote of his own sorrow at the death of his friend Scipio: "I have been bereaved of a friend," he said, "such as the world will never see again. . . . (But) I do not feel that Scipio has suffered any misfortune; I am the one who has suffered misfortune."

To have a friend is to acknowledge that some part of someone else's life which we have held tenderly, trustingly in our own hands might well die with us. Where does grief for the dead come from, in fact, if not from the anger and sense of abandonment that emerges from the realization that some part of ourselves has been taken away from us without our permission? Grief is simply a measure of the joy, the depth that comes from growing to know another and letting her know me in ways in which I am exposed to no one else.

Indeed, to lose a friend is to be cast back into the insularism that is the self. It is a dark and sniveling place to be. It is a dangerous place to be, narrow and confined by the limits of the self. Only friendship can really save us from our own smallness.

But first, of course, there are things to consider: What exactly is a friend? Is friendship really possible? Is friendship a necessary good or simply a social filler? Is friendship spiritual? Isn't God alone enough? What, if anything, does friendship have to do with living life forever on the brink of becoming?

There is a long answer and a short one to the question of what friendship has to do with personal development and spiritual growth. The short answer is, "Everything"—if, that is, we are to believe the thinkings of the philosophers, the findings of modern social scientists, as well as the witness of history and the wisdom of Ecclesiastes. The long answer comes in the slowly dawning awareness that once we are loved we have an obligation to live as best we can. Once we have discovered the love that doubles life but does not consume it, we must live so that the other, who walks by the light within us as well as the light within herself, may not proceed befuddled by our own failure to illuminate the way. The love of a friend comes always with a lantern in hand.

By love I am not talking about passion, though that

will certainly, in one energizing sense or another, be a fortifying dimension of any deep and good relationship. By love I am talking about the process of melting into the life of another in ways that fuse our souls, open our hearts, and stretch our minds, and all the while claiming nothing in return. Friendship is the process of opening ourselves to the care, to the wisdom, of the other. The love of friendship is the love that holds no secrets, has no unasked questions, no unspoken thoughts, no unanswered concerns. Friendship extends us into places we have not gone before and cannot go alone.

Friendship may be either ultimate or commonplace, but it is never without the gain of a little more self.

The history of friendship has been an obscure one in every dimension, but most of all, for women. In the manner of just about everything else in life, friendship has been a male preserve. Montaigne, as late as the sixteenth century, wrote in his essay "On Friendship" that ". . . the normal capacity of women is, in fact, unequal to the demands of that communion and intercourse on which the sacred bond (of friendship) is fed; their souls do not seem firm enough to bear the strain of so hard and lasting a tie." Montaigne was not original, not isolated, in his thinking. He had centuries of philosophy and male discourse on which to base his statement.

The ancients—Plato and Aristotle and the schools of philosophy to follow them—assumed that friendship was one of the higher acts of the human soul and that males, the highest creature in the hierarchy of creation, would choose their equals—other males—to be their friends. Friends were the glue of the nation, the network of political allies, associations, loyalties, and collaborations on which rested the decisions of the state.

Cicero, the great Roman orator, wrote his classic essay "On Friendship" not as a tribute to personal affection but as a final attempt to save the failing republic of Rome from encroaching monarchy and dictatorship by reviving democratic networks that rested on shared ideals, on personal relationships.

In the Middle Ages the word "friend" included relatives as well as any associates or benefactors or public patrons who could be counted on for the alliances it might take to secure the power and property of the family. Friends were, for the most part in this society, simply "connections." Since such political concerns were not the realm of women and since most women were confined to the arena of the family, neither was friendship a woman's domain. In fact, only in our own time has the privatization of friendship become common social currency.

And yet, it is equally true that there is throughout history another, deeper, more personal tradition of spiritual friendship than the alliances of the court and the castle. There is another current—plain for us to see —running parallel to this political dimension. There is another model of friendship, besides the conventional model of male friendship, from which we can draw to measure the quality of our own, if we only have the eyes to see it.

Philosophers and leaders in the spiritual life wrestled with the idea of friendship from century to century. Aristotle stated, "What is a friend? A single soul dwelling in two bodies." And Catullus, in one of the most moving eulogies to a friend ever given, said of the relationship, "Our soul is buried, mine with yours entwined." No mere political connections here.

The desert monastics understood the role of spiritual friendship and considered it an essential part of the spiritual life even when they exalted *apathaeia*—passionlessness—and warned against the distractions of human attachments. The mandate of hospitality brought these women and men to attend to the physical as well as the spiritual needs of those whom they saw as their spiritual disciples.

St. Ambrose saw human friendship as a necessary part of the outpouring of God's friendship. "Because God is true," Ambrose argued, "friends can be true.... Because God offers friendship, we can be each other's friends."

St. Augustine assumed community and human relationships as the ground of growth. "The more friends I shall have," he wrote, "the more can we love wisdom in common."

And St. Benedict considered the manifestation of the self to another as a fundamental step on the path to full human development.

The tradition was an unfailing one: friendship became the mucilage of the Christian community and reached its high point in the spiritual writings of the Cistercian monk and abbot Aelred of Riveaulx, who dedicated his life to the subject. In the twelfth century he wrote a theology of friendship that derived from the thesis that "God is friendship." To Aelred, friendship was a necessary dimension of the Christian life and a particular dimension of an individual's spiritual awareness, as well.

These views of the spiritual life did not, in the long run, prevail. In a world dominated by war, famine, plague, and oppression, the God of Love lost out to God the Judge and Jesus the Lord. Negative asceticism, repentance, constraint—all designed to atone for the kind of sin that could generate such godly wrath— remained the temper of the time. During the same period, with the rise of the all-male university system, the influence of women on idea development and their public visibility diminished even more. Cut off from the growing academic world, whatever experiences, whatever insights, women could have brought to the subject were lost behind the cloistered walls of convents and castles and kitchens. Friendship went its chauvinist way, the stuff of male poets and essayists, perhaps, but not the coin of the realm and definitely not a woman's prerogative.

Until now. Until our time. Until, that is, the release of energy that came with women's new awareness of themselves led women to speak of their own experiences. Until psychology began the analysis of human relationships and discovered, lo and behold, that relationship was of the essence of being woman. Until we discovered the place of talk in the development of human community and a woman's healing gift for it. Then we began to look back on history with new eyes. Then we began to see, as if for the first time, the women who had mothered our hopes and had proclaimed their presence as women and had demonstrated their connection to each other and to God. Then we began to see one another with new eyes. Then we discovered what it was to be a woman with other women. "Each friend," Anais Nin writes, "represents a world in us, a world possibly not born until they arrive, and it is only by this meeting that a new world is born."

Friendship in general, women's friendships in particular, has become a topic of value again. Friendship is coming to life in a new way today. And it is coming to life so clearly in women. The question is, what qualities sustain it and where shall we look to find them if we are to live all the worlds for which we have been made? Women themselves tell us now what they look for in friendship—and scripture shows us instances where these very qualities in women have changed the world. It is time to honor both of them.

"My friends are my estate," wrote Emily Dickinson. Friends are, in other words, the only wealth I will have at the end. My friends will be the treasure I accrue in life and a measure, perhaps, of my own worth as well. It is surely, then, of the highest spiritual order to celebrate the Sacrament of Friendship.

LYDIA

Growth

"No soul is desolate," George Eliot wrote, "as long as there is a human being for whom it can feel trust and reverence." The comment deserves serious consideration. It brings us to rethink the whole notion of friendship. If Eliot is correct, then a friendship is more than an element of social life. It is a spiritual force that touches the soul.

The fact is that companionship is not enough to fill a life. What is needed in human relationships above all, if they are to give substance to our lives, is the quality of fusion, the character of meld. It is the challenge of connection. It is an insight of grave consequence in a world where we can live in crowds forever and never even notice that we are alone. It is so easy to think that we have friends and know how to be a friend when all we really have are contacts. It is so easy to think we have a relationship with someone when all we really have is more or less time for idle conversations with people we see often but keep at a distance always.

Where there is no reverence, no trust, there may be attraction, but there is no friendship. It is a social question of great import in the highly anonymous society in which we live, where neighbors do not know neighbors and telephones have answering machines to weed out calls.

The underlying tension in contemporary Western society is the struggle between the public and the personal. We are a private people who happen to live in groups. We are individuals who develop communities based more on the rights of each separate member than on our obligations to the groups themselves. We prize autonomy as we honor little else, and yet nothing has become more apparent in the advance toward personal independence than the inextricable connection between human relationship and mental health. Women who have friends—who trust and reverence someone—are simply healthier, happier people. They're more responsive to others, more secure about themselves. Friends open new worlds for us and invite us in, laughing and singing. Friends carry our burdens in their own hearts and give us the wisdom of distance to deal with them. Friends, the people we really trust, point a way.

The question is how to balance independence and relationship. What is required for us to come out of ourselves without at the same time losing ourselves in the interests and ideas, the plans and pursuits of the other? It's a difficult question in a society of gurus who offer new feel-good fixes by the day. But whatever the latest fashion in self-development, there is always, for the woman who looks for root in the tried-and-true, the memory of Lydia. To understand friendship and its place in the life of a woman, we need to maintain the memory of Lydia.

———⊶⊷———

Lydia, whom scripture credits, along with Paul, for the implantation of Christianity in Europe, is clearly a strong and independent woman, unusual for her time. Unusual perhaps for any time. The knowledge we have about the woman Lydia may be sparse—but it is clear. She was a woman of substance. She was strong-minded, and she was self-directing.

There is no mention of a husband in the scripture that describes Lydia, no mention of family chores, no hint of dependence. No sheltered small-town girl, this one. On the contrary. Lydia came from a bustling commercial area bordering on the Aegean once itself called "Lydia." It was an urban gateway between East and West, a crossroads of ideas, cultures, and business. Lydia had experience. She had traveled. She knew more about life than the boundaries of the clan and the certainties of the countryside. Lydia had seen things of which most women of her time had never even dreamed. And she gathered these women around her and opened to them a whole new way of thinking about the world.

Lydia was, the scripture says, "a seller of purple." She did business, in other words, with the kind of people who made clothes for kings or dyes for local industries. She was not a street vendor. She was not a hired hand. This woman had influence, and she used it. She "constrained" Paul, the epistle points out, to stay in her house, to make his first congregation in Europe a congregation of women. Lydia was not the average woman.

She was, in fact, just the kind of woman anyone would want for a friend. She was someone to be looked up to, someone whose timbre could be reckoned. Lydia did what she set out to do. Lydia could be trusted.

In the Lydias of the world lies the self-confidence that magnetizes others, that draws people to them, that gives a sense of security and a touch of excitement to the lives of those around them. She was a seeker who swept others along in the passion of her pursuits and made the going worthwhile if for no other reason than the exhilaration of the search. She was a free woman who freed other women around her. In Lydia, a woman could see what she herself wanted to become. She could develop a sense of belonging. She could explore new notions in safe space and without disdain.

The Lydia dimension of friendship is the desire to draw from another the strength we need to go beyond where we would ever go alone. We search for a Lydia in our lives to give us the courage to walk on tightropes above raging cataracts of confusion below us. With Lydias to lead the way, we can do anything. We can open ourselves to new ideas and risk the beckoning unknown.

There is a problem with looking for a Lydia, however. The role of Lydia is to lead us beyond herself. When we find ourselves walking only in the shadow of the Lydias in our lives rather than beside them we have substituted dependence for friendship. It is so easy to mistake one for the other, but the signs are clear. The real Lydias, when we finally find them, are not those who remake us in their image. They are those who enable us to become the best of what we can be, to develop who we are in ourselves, the ones who see our ideas as just as valuable, just as possible, as their own. The Lydias around us don't enslave us to their ideas. They provide the environment, the model, that leads us to think on our own. In that kind of strength lies the glory of friendship.

PRISCA

Self

"Never contract friendship," Confucius said, "with anyone who is not better than yourself." The idea may be sound, but, given its ancient origin, it must be at least suspect, if not spurious. The problem is that friendship as social convention has changed from one age to the other. In ancient Greece, the friend was a political ally. In medieval Europe to talk about friendship was, in large part, really to be making a comment on the solidarity of the extended family. It meant patronage. In some ages and cultures it was understood as comradeship or some kind of institutionalized formal relations between families. Clearly, the intentions across the ages to choose for a friend someone who was superior were guided by various motives and various meanings. But not now.

In our time, thanks to the focus on the individual and personal development, the idea of friendship has become part of the subject of the self. Friendship—what we mean by it, how we deal with it—at this time, in this society, has to do with what it means to be me. My friends become an extension of myself. They reflect what I think about, what I want in life, what has meaning to me, what kind of depth I have. The truth is that the friends we make have something to do with the women we are, the human beings we are becoming.

Whatever Confucius's motives may have been in advising people of his time to look for friends in whom they could recognize qualities superior to their own, the advice has its own kind of value now. In an age in which we live like strangers in a strange world, far from family ties, borne along from one shifting institution to another, friendship ceases to be simply a series of social contacts and instead becomes some kind of lifeline. Friends become our substitutes for the families, the institutions, the ideas we have been forced—for whatever reasons—to leave behind. Today the words of Confucius take on added meaning. Today we realize that we have to determine what it is to be superior and what it means for the shaping of our own lives. Today the memory of Prisca becomes spiritual injunction.

Prisca was a woman who knew hardship and survived it. When the emperor Claudius drove the Jews out of Rome, around 40 CE, she had been forced to leave everyone she knew, to relinquish everything she held dear, to forego all the security, all the warmth that the familiar gives. She was a refugee in a stable society, forced to begin again, required against her will to start life over in new territory with new people. She had been uprooted, displaced, left to fend for herself in a society where kinship was key to security. And she survived it all. She even reached out to take other outcasts in.

It is in Corinth that Prisca and her husband, Aquila, two tentmakers, meet another tentmaker, Paul of Tarsus, who is making a second missionary journey to areas outside of Judea. They open their home to him, scripture says, and for two years, travel with him as missionaries themselves, begin the first house church in Corinth and, sure of the truth they feel in their hearts, contest with Apollos in Ephesus, a speaker of no small skill but limited background who has been teaching in the local synagogue—and they "instruct him more accurately." She is teacher, leader, missionary, all traits that have emerged where they would be least likely to be found: in a refugee, a tentmaker and a woman.

And what does that have to do with my choice of friends? More, perhaps, than I have ever realized. Prisca is mentioned six times in scripture, four of them prior to the naming of her husband, the kind of recognition that is unheard of for a woman of the time. Prisca is, in other words, a person in her own right. Prisca is not defined by anything or anyone around her or outside of her. Whatever her own lack of supports, of firm ground on which to take her place in the security of the system around her, she speaks her own truth in her own name, and she is respected for it.

Prisca is the sign of all the untapped resources within the coarsest craters of the human heart. In her I recognize the one who has the capacity to draw from the well of the self when there is every reason in the world to believe that the well must be dry.

The Prisca dimension of friendship is the dream of finding in myself the same kind of hidden qualities that I have recognized in another. It is the choice to mine myself to the depth, beyond the limits of what I am inclined to think are the boundaries of my existence. The woman Prisca—exiled, unlettered, simple— reminds me to value the friend who has talents I seek but have yet to develop. She is the prism through which I can catch sight of my own better self.

There is a thin line, however, between admiring what I know to be superior to myself and giving way to the despair that the superiority of another can engender. It takes great strength to be a self in the shadow of those whose self seems, at first sight, to be so much greater than my own. But unless I aspire to develop the best qualities of the best people around me, I am doomed either to stay what I am or to seek out the companionship of those who can only ignore my limitations or, worse, validate them. "Tell me what company you keep," Cervantes said, "and I'll tell you what you are." To be our best selves we must keep company with those whom we ourselves know to be better than we are.

Friendship is the sacrament of possibility. It is trusting that those for whom I care and who say they care for me will reveal to me what I cannot see in myself and prod it to its fullness. The Lydias of our lives stretch the self; the Priscas of our lives confirm the self.

The search for the superior in others is the search for the superior in myself. It is the magnet in the heart that leads me to aspire to levels higher than the watermarks of the culture in which I have been bred. My friend is the one who shows me what I, too, can become if I only set myself to be it.

DEBORAH

Wisdom

"The rule of friendship," the Buddha said, "means there should be mutual sympathy between them, each supplying what the other lacks and trying to benefit the other...." The words ring true. Friendship is not as much a matter of happenstance as we are inclined to think.

Perhaps one of life's most precious lessons is that we must learn to choose our friends as well as to find them. The corollary of the insight, of course, is that we must learn not to allow ourselves simply to fall into alliances and acquaintanceships that come and go like starlight on the water, exciting for a while but easily forgotten. We must learn, in other words, not to make life a playground of faceless, nameless people—all of whom are useful for awhile but who never really touch the soul or stretch the mind or prod the conscience.

On the contrary, the realization that friendship is one of the great spiritual resources of human existence drives us beyond the superficial to the meaningful. It leads us to create relationships that count for something, rather than to simply wander from one casual social affair to another.

It may, in fact, be the friends we make who most accurately measure the depth of our own souls. For that we are each responsible.

To grow, then, requires that we provide for ourselves the kinds of relationships that demand more of us than continual immersion in the mundane. It requires us to surround ourselves with people who speak to the best part of us from the best part of themselves. It means that we must actively seek out as friends those who have something worth saying. And then we must learn to listen well to them so that they can hone our own best intuitions, challenge our least profound assumptions, point out directions that take us to another level of thought and care and determination.

Then, at times when life is most unclear, most confusing, we need Deborah's wisdom, her quality of friendship. But only an awareness of our own limitations can possibly prepare us for it.

———∞∞∞———

Deborah, one of the judges of Israel, sat under the palm trees outside the city, scripture records, "and judged people." They brought their questions to her for answers. They brought their confusions to her for enlightenment. They brought their fears to her for calming. And she listened to them. But, like any good friend, she did more than listen.

"A friend," Cicero wrote, "is, as it were, a second

self." The Deborahs in our lives know us as well as we know ourselves. The difference is that they also help us see beyond ourselves.

Deborah was a judge in Israel because they recognized her wisdom even when they doubted their own. They knew that she saw through them as if she were reading her own motives. She read their hearts as if she were hearing her own. She understood their struggles because she had been through them herself. And, wise woman that she was, she helped them find the next step in life—the one they knew they had to take—even when they understood it least.

Israel, after twenty years of foreign oppression, liberated itself because its people had the sense to know what they did not know—they trusted Deborah. They trusted a wisdom beyond their own, and they did what she told them to do, however unlikely, however dangerous it was.

During Deborah's time, a century or so after the Israelite entry into Canaan, the area was controlled by King Jabin of Hazor. Deborah summoned the warrior Barak, a good man but too unsure of himself to risk an attempt to free the Israelite people on his own impulse.

Deborah, who knew the sufferings of the people, recognized his abilities and instructed him to take ten thousand troops and confront Jabin's general, Sisera, and his army's nine hundred iron chariots, on Mount Tabor.

"If you come with me, I will go," Barak told her. "If not, I will not go."

And Deborah answered, "I will go with you," and then, removing all doubt that she wasn't a realist about the nature of her society and its low regard for the ideas or stature of women, she added: "However, there will be no glory for you in the course you are taking, for then the Lord will deliver Sisera into the hands of a woman."

The story provides a focal point into our own private worlds, even now. It says something about both our own needs and the needs of the world around us.

First, we learn that when we lose trust in ourselves, only the trust of another can possibly save us and stretch us beyond our own low self-esteem.

Second, we learn the even subtler truth that the wise not only know what is happening—but also why it is happening. Deborah knew what most of the world has yet to learn: when we diminish the role of women's experience and insight in our world, we diminish the needs and humanity of men as well.

We need wisdom figures in our lives because facts are not enough. Wisdom sees more than facts. Wisdom understands motives and reasons and results. Deborah reminds us that smart friends and cute friends, talented friends and friends of high status are no substitute for those who have wisdom.

But that means deliberately placing ourselves in the trust of those friends whose values and insights are clear. It requires us to look for them carefully—as we would for anyone we felt to be essential to either our physical or our mental health.

Life is short, and energies are limited. Friendship requires time and care. To waste these resources on relationships that bring no depth, no vision, is to waste a valuable part of life—a part that changes over time as it grows from the need for self-disclosure to the proof of authenticity. To be wise ourselves, then, we must make whatever effort it takes to find the Deborah among our friends.

PHOEBE

Support

"Friendship," Kahlil Gibran wrote, "is always a sweet responsibility, never an opportunity." To the person who goes through life making the "connections" that promise the right committee appointments, guarantee the plum promotions, or assure the regular invitations to all the best cocktail parties of life, Gibran's observation is a confusing one. After all, isn't the purpose of making the right friends to get to the right places and meet the right people? The two positions—Gibran's spiritual dictum and society's pragmatic one—reflect two very distinct worldviews, both of them real, both of them true to a certain degree. But the snag in the game of friendship is that the word "friend" itself is so often used so loosely.

Unfortunately, friendship comes in varieties that merge and blur, confuse and contradict one another. A friend is, to many, any of a battery of things: an acquaintance, an associate, a comrade, a compatriot, a childhood companion, an adult peer, a longstanding fellow traveler in a common enterprise. Obviously, the real character of any friendship depends on the mind of the person who is defining it. Contemporary research has divided and subdivided friendships into a number of different levels, from "best friend" to "casual acquaintance," from "friendships of commitment" to "friendships of convenience." Clearly, to say "We've been friends for years" is to say everything and to say nothing at the same time.

So how do we tell one kind of friendship from the other? And, in the end, does it make any difference? Really? After all, friendships among women have never been much defined under any circumstances. The classic literature of past eras all record myths of heroic male friendships: Achilles and Patroclus, each of whom fought on behalf of the other; Damon and Pythias, who begged to die for one another; David and Jonathan, who loved each other despite the fact that Saul, Jonathan's father, sought to kill David; Aelred and Richard, twelfth-century Cistercian monks who reshaped the thinking of medieval monasticism on the spiritual dimensions of friendship. The relationship of man-to-man was a given—but not even the fairy tales recalled great friendships among women. The point was clear: Women did not need women friends. Women needed men.

Not until the mid-1970s did the academic world even bother to ask in any scientific way whether or not women had friendships at all. As late as 1969, in fact, the social scientist Lionel Tiger argued that women were not genetically programmed to bond with one another. But then the floodgates opened. Human development departments everywhere began to study the character and role of friendships among women. The findings completely reversed the philosophical assumptions of so many centuries. Researchers found a clear connection between women's better health, longer life span, resistance to stress, and successful life transitions to the presence of close, confidante relationships in their lives. By 1984, social scientists were suggesting that friendships between women actually maintain marital structures by enabling the women to create personal space and autonomy within the family arena, and historians were now studying the woman-to-woman bond that had created convents, mobilized women's social resistance groups, sustained women in harems, and built Beguinages in Europe. But how can any of it be explained? The answer is getting clearer every day: what bonds women is the enduring echo of Phoebe in every woman's soul. In Phoebe is the seed of great friendship, deep feeling.

Phoebe gets only two lines in all of scripture, and they are, at first glance, apparently innocuous ones. Paul says of her by way of introducing her to the fledgling little church in Rome to whom Phoebe has traveled hundreds of miles to deliver Paul's epistle, "I commend to you our sister Phoebe, a deacon of the church at Cenchreae, so that you may welcome her in the Lord as is fitting for the saints, and help her in whatever she may require from you, for she has been a benefactor of many and of myself as well."

Phoebe was a "deacon"—one who serves, a "sister"—one who loves, and "a benefactor"—one who lives to support the dreams of others and which she makes her own. Phoebe was, in other words, a loving presence, a selfless doer, an altruist of souls. She poured her life out on others like oil from an alabaster jar. She healed and served and cared and carried all the burdens of all the people around her. Phoebe freed people to be who they were by attending to what they themselves needed. And she did it at great cost to herself. She "put herself out," as we might say. She gave herself away.

The Phoebe element in friendship is the quiet constancy that gives life its composition. The Phoebes of life hold the world together. These are the friends who never miss sending your birthday card, who call "just to see how you are," who bring the casserole when you're tired, who take the children for a ride to give you some time to yourself, who listen while you talk, who help you hold up your end of the sky.

The Phoebe dimension of friendship requires us to be self-contained: she became an independent woman, but not self-centered. She did not become herself for her own sake only. Phoebe reminds us that we do not exist for ourselves alone—but she does not call us to efface ourselves. She simply compels us to be about more than ourselves. Friendship, we see in Phoebe, obligates us to the good of the other but at the same time does not deny us the obligation to be the fullness of the self.

"Trouble shared is trouble halved," Dorothy Sayers wrote. The Phoebes in our lives call us to be conscious of the needs around us. When asked, women say repeatedly that a friend "is someone I can call on for help."

The Phoebes make the world a better place, a compassionate place, a place where friendship flourishes.

Phoebe is a warning as well as a witness. She calls us to realize that to be like her is not to be a sycophant. Phoebe does not live to defer. She was a "deacon," an identified minister of the church. She is not a member of some eternal servant class. She is not the "female female" whose lot in life is to be the caretaker of the human race because she is not able to do anything else. Phoebe is the friend who—by being the one we need when we need her—reminds us that our own gifts of self are meant to be developed for the sake of the universe. The Phoebe quality of friendship reminds us that we are not servants; we, too, are raised up to be co-creators of the cosmos we call life.

ESTHER

Leadership

"A true friend," Emerson wrote," is somebody who can make us do what we can." Perhaps no better definition of leadership has ever been written. But, unfortunately, it doesn't get much notice.

Leadership has always been more associated with power and authority than with understanding and friendship. It has been misused to get people to do what we want rather than what they can. Meeting the wishes of the leader, history implies, has always been much more common, much more important, than encouraging the talents of the ones led.

Maybe that's why the very idea of the leadership of women has also always been considered a kind of oxymoron—like hot ice, or deafening silence. Leadership, we have been taught to assume for so long, was—like so much else—a male prerogative. Women, men decided, were too mild, too compliant, too docile, not "manly" enough, to lead.

But, ironically enough, history itself debunks that kind of prejudice, that kind of self-serving propaganda. The truth is that women leaders have launched some of the most impacting movements in history: Queen Boudicca, in 60 CE, led the revolt against the Romans that almost drove them out of Britain. Empress Theodora, in the sixth century CE, closed the brothels of Byzantium and led the fight against the imprisonment of prostitutes while the men they serviced went free. Trotula, a physician of the medical school of Salerno in 1000 CE, began one of the earliest studies of gynecology. Teresa of Avila reformed religious life. Emily Pankhurst brought the attention of the world to a woman's right to vote. Mother Jones organized women workers and developed an entire labor movement. Dorothy Day led the Catholic Worker Movement. Simone de Beauvoir brought the world to understand the nature of structural oppression. Betty Friedan ignited the emergence of Second Wave feminism. And all of them led, not for the sake of their own advantage, not for the sake of power or money or prestige, but always for the sake of the other, of their friends—and at whatever cost to themselves.

There is no doubt about it—women are definitely leaders. But they lead differently. Their goal is not to force people to do anything. Their goal is to lead people to do what is best for everyone. They do not function as enemies of a common good. They do not raise armies. They do not kill the opposition. Instead they seek to stop the oppression. They seek to empower the people they serve. They arrive at major decisions, not as enemies of the opposition, but as friend to everyone involved.

Many women today point to the work of earlier generations of women as having borne the pressure and the ignominy that went with breaking paths for women in traditionally male-defined arenas. Those efforts in the past, they know, count a lot in their own lives and in the lives of women at large.

As Jean Paul Richter wrote, "Every friend is to the other a sun, and a sunflower also." They both attract and follow. The message from women—for women— has always been clear: the work of women leaders was meant to benefit not only themselves but generations of women to follow, generations of people to come.

Rather than simply bask in their own talents and skills, women and friends today celebrate each and every Esther moment in history—moments in which women spoke out for others without fear, and by doing so, changed the world.

Queen Esther remains a compelling exemplar of power wielded by the powerless in favor of those even more powerless than they.

Esther, a young Jewish woman, after having been chosen as queen by the gentile King Ahasuerus, found herself torn between assuring her own safety in a palace poised to destroy all the Jews in the kingdom, and using her position for the sake of the survival of her people.

Esther lived in an autocratic world where the king ruled by fiat, where his last queen had been deposed for not obeying his orders, and where the chief minister who had engineered the royal decree calling for the extinction of the Jewish community in the kingdom was rabidly anti-Semitic.

To be on the wrong side of a patriarchal, oppressive system such as this meant that to fight it, a person had to be prepared either to wage war or to face death. Esther could not wage war, and the death of errant women was already far too common.

Effectiveness in such a system depended, Esther knew, on being able to wield ruthless power ruthlessly. She also knew she had neither the royal status nor the raw power to demand anything. She was queen, not a royal advisor, not minister of the realm.

When Esther's uncle, Mordecai, appealed to her for help, she sent a stark and simple message: "All the king's servants and the people of the king's provinces know that if any man or woman goes to the king inside the inner court without being called, there is but one law—all alike are to be put to death. Only if the king holds out the golden scepter to someone, may that person live. I myself have not been called to come in to the king for thirty days."

When they told Mordecai what Esther had said, Mordecai told them to reply to Esther, "Do not think that in the king's palace you will escape any more than all the other Jews. For if you keep silence at such a time as this, relief and deliverance will rise for the Jews from another quarter, but you and your father's family will perish. Who knows? Perhaps you have come to royal dignity for just such a time as this."

Suddenly, Esther understood what leadership really meant, and she replied: "Go, gather all the Jews to be found in Susa, and hold a fast on my behalf, and neither eat nor drink for three days, night or day. I and my maids will also fast as you do. After that I will go to the king, though it is against the law; and if I perish, I perish."

The stakes were plain: This was a king who disposed of people—even queens—casually. To speak out unbidden in favor of those already condemned could only be foolhardy.

Then Esther did a man's job a woman's way. She did not seek power over the opposition. Instead she set out to make the king a friend. She sought the cooperation it takes to change oppression, rather than simply thwart it. She exposed the plot that planned to wipe out all Jews from the kingdom; she sought the king's understanding; she gained his support. She demonstrated the damage that would be done to the king himself if such an inhuman act were carried out under his seal of approval. Finally, she integrated Jews into the very court that was going to destroy them, and, in this way, she changed the society without either destroying or dividing it.

The Esther quality of friendship can change a war-torn world, can bring peace, can engage the whole world into one common human enterprise, can link the world rather than entangle it in the endless search for power and superiority.

But for that to happen we must permit it, develop it, encourage it, and value it in our women friends. For that to happen, we must all rediscover Esther—her integrity, her courage, her willingness to embrace the whole world. We must all find friends who are both sun and sunflowers, who lead us on but who are just as open to our own leadership.

MARTHA OF BETHANY

Truth

"When a woman tells the truth," Adrienne Rich writes, "she creates the possibility for more truth around her." And Plutarch, many centuries before, agreed. "I want a friend," he said, "who will follow me only in obedience to truth." It is a hard saying. It takes all the marshmallow, all the frills out of human relationships. It brings human communion to the bar of nobility. It is the first principle of real friendship.

Those who prattle conventional wisdom but never speak their own are dangerous people to have around. To call one of them "friend" is worse. If we really believed that such parroting were of the essence of friendship, we could be inclined to trust them. But women don't. One of the most clearly defined dimensions of friendship by women is a sense of reliable alliance and the opportunity to obtain guidance. Women want more in a friend, in other words, than someone with whom they can simply idle away some time. They want someone on whom they can count and someone who will tell them the truth.

Truth is a strange thing, however. It has as many definitions, as many shades, as friendship itself. There is a truth that can be counted up, for instance. But the fact that a thousand people like chocolate and one does not may well be a mathematical truth but one that is at best incomplete. What is the real truth of the statement: that chocolate is universally good—or that it is not equally satisfactory to everyone? The question is a crucial one if truth is really to be honored and friendship is really to be true.

There is a difference between fact and truth. The problem is that for far too long, perhaps, much of what is only fact has been allowed to pass for the fullness of truth. It is facile to allow one facet of the truth to speak for all the truth about a subject. Truth has many faces. There is truth that can be tested and found to be either true or false. There is the truth of history and the truth of tradition and the truth of authority and the truth of social expectations. Indeed, there are facts aplenty to press down upon a woman's head. But there is very little of a woman's truth that has been dignified by its inclusion in the pantheon of ethical realities. Instead, women have been told for centuries what others—men—said was sin for women and good for women and necessary for women and essential to women and then told that it was all truth. It was true, women were told, that to refuse conjugal relations was sin for them, that self-sacrifice was good for them, that obedience to men was necessary for them, and that the modesty defined by men was essential to their integrity.

The fact is that many men sincerely thought so. The truth is also, however, that many women knew otherwise but were never asked. Indeed, unless the facts pressed down upon a woman are a woman's truth as well, it is at best a truth that is pitifully partial.

But another truth keeps roiling around in the human psyche, disappearing only to reemerge from century to century in women. This is more truth than they have been traditionally told. Now women want to know a woman's truth. They want to hear from women who do not like chocolate. They have come to realize that just because we have a fact that is true does not mean that it holds universal truth.

Women are beginning to value the truth, the experience, of other women. They are beginning to recognize the cry of Martha of Bethany.

───⌘───

Martha of Bethany knew both fact and truth. She knew for a fact that women were not allowed to study the Torah, and when she watched Jesus instruct Mary in the Torah, she let both of them understand that she was seeing the tradition of exclusion crumbled by them. She also knew the truth. On the road to Bethany, just as surely as Peter made a confession of faith in Jesus as messiah, it was Martha who said to Jesus, "I know that you are the messiah." Her experience had told her what the rabbis would not admit. Her insights had penetrated what the eyes of the system did not see. Her heart had heard what the ears of the pharisees could not hear. Martha of Bethany was a truth-teller.

The Martha quality of friendship makes it plain that women have a truth to tell that is their own. It gives a woman the confidence it takes to claim her own experience and it leads her to seek out, to trust, the truths inside the women around her. Martha of Bethany calls women to see themselves as architects of the faith as well as its consumers.

It is truth in a friendship that gives it depth, and truth that makes it whole. It is truth that drives us to explore ourselves as well as the other, the other as well as ourselves. Truth makes possible the exposure of the soul and the riches of experience. It validates a person's life. What I have come to know may not be universal knowledge, if there is any such thing, but it is my knowledge—and that is more than enough to kindle my growing, and the growth of others as well.

The dark side of truth is brutality, a word unkindly, untimely said. It is often inflicted in the name of friendship but must never be confused with it. Brutality is never truth. It is, at best, the petty side of a fact. Most of all, brutality is never the stuff of friendship. Oliver Wendell Holmes wrote, "Leave your friend to learn unpleasant things from enemies; they are ready enough to tell them." There are those who would argue that it is precisely the function of friendship to be the bearer of the hostile and the scathing. But there is already too much of that in life to claim for it a role in the rank of friendship. The function of the one who loves me is to enable me to bear the hard truth, to cope with it, to learn from it, and to survive it. *Not* to be the first to say it. "A friend," a Near East proverb teaches, "is one who warns you."

The Martha dimension of friendship brings a woman's experience out of the dark night of oblivion into the clear light of new understanding. It brings women to the point of dignity and gives dignity to women. Any woman who honors the truth within her frees the woman she calls friend to discover for herself what is behind the next question, the next absolute, the next order, the next sin that is committed in the name of God. Any friendship that carries the truths of life is surely a holy one.

VERONICA

Presence

"What is the opposite of two?"
Richard Wilbur pondered. "A lonely me; a
lonely you." There may be no more
poignant line in literature. The very
thought of finding ourselves alone, cut off
from the touch of a warm hand, left without a strong shoulder, bereft of the presence of the one who matters, terrifies us to

the core. Who of us really wants to go into the darkness of pain or hurt or fear alone? Who of us really wants to go into the light of joy and celebration alone?

Whatever the romantic images of the strong and self-sufficient heroes, of solitary and separated hermits, of isolated and rugged individualists, the truth is that, somehow, somewhere, in the end, the human community takes everything to itself. "Alone we can do so little; together we can do so much," Helen Keller said. We exist only in connection with the rest of the human race. We cannot stand alone. And yet, far too often we do.

We find ourselves alone in times of great stress, of great loss, of great personal pressure. We find ourselves in that spiritual space inside the self where no other can possibly come. Much as we would want them to do otherwise. Much as we try to communicate with the other, there is a wall of solid glass between us, apparently translucent but really opaque. Then we may look like we have touched another life, but the touch, whatever its sincerity, is false. Every time we find ourselves saying, "What I'm trying to say is . . ." or "No, what I mean is . . ." or "Why can't you understand what I'm saying?" or "Are you listening to me?" we are alone. Frightfully, irrevocably alone.

Men often use solitude to prove their manliness, to stake their bragging rights. Women never bluster about solitude. They can accept it in all the empty kitchens of the world. They can endure it through long, dark, frightening nights. But they seldom, if ever, choose it, they never glorify it, and they always seek to fill it. Whatever can be done together can be borne. What must be done alone is near impossible. For women, relationships—presence to the other—are of the essence of existence, the answer to isolation, the very marrow of their meaning.

There is in women's friendships a different quality of presence. Men, very often, conduct their friendships "side-by-side," in shared activities, in project development, in group play, in situations that bring no basic threat to power and demand no emotional vulnerability. Women, on the other hand, shape their relationships "face-to-face," in mutual dependence, in honest conversation, in exposures of personal weaknesses.

Women carry within them to everyone they meet the power of Veronica.

⸺◦◦◦⸺

Veronica is a figment of the scriptures of the mind, a kind of Christian midrash on the Way of the Cross. There, centuries of oral tradition tell us, a woman by the name of Veronica looked on the bruised and bleeding body of Jesus as he struggled his cross up Golgotha alone. Then, in a burst of anguish for the pain she could not tolerate a second longer, she lunged out of the crowd, through the guard, and with a grandiose gesture of unmitigated compassion for the wounds of another, wiped away the blood on his face with a sweep of her own veil.

The Veronica story is midrash, true, but that is not to say that it is nothing. Midrash, Judaism teaches us, is what the heart knows has gone on between the lines of scripture that scripture did not detail for the mind: Noah's fear, Abraham's confusion, Miriam's jubilation over the rescue of Moses, Joseph's anxiety, Mary's determination, Veronica's empathic presence. They all live clearly, certainly in the human heart, the truth for which no truth is needed. Veronica is the awareness in the Christian unconscious that "face-to-face" women face down pain. "Show me a friend who will weep with me," the Yugoslavian proverb teaches. "Those who will laugh with me I can find myself."

The Veronica quality of friendship is itself a powerful one. Women look to other women to be the understanding, the empathy, the presence they need in matters of the heart too important to be overlooked in the process of living, too small to be noticed by the male world. Veronica the friend takes off her own veil, exposes herself in society, to be a balm where there is only ache. Veronica does not pretend to solve the problem, but she refuses to ignore it. She makes herself a clear and contradictory presence to the oppressive power structures around her, a confidante of impenetrable silence, a keeper of secrets, an anchor in the wind.

Women who know the call of Veronica in their relationships give great attention to the other without benefit of possessiveness or pettiness or expectations. Maude Preston writes of the experience, "There isn't much that I can do, but I can sit an hour with you, and I can share a joke with you, and sometimes share reverses, too, as on our way we go."

With the Veronicas of friendship, it is the staying power that counts, the awareness of awareness that carries a woman from one hard moment to another with an uplifting arm, an open mind. Women see a woman-friend as an equal, not as a partner who must be coaxed or coddled or persuaded or coerced before they can be made to listen, to understand. A woman-friend is the one to whom a woman turns to understand the gravity of all the trivia of her life.

The Veronicas in our lives bring the power of affirmation to our pain. They confirm its reality, its injustice, and, in the end, its ultimate resolvability. With a Veronica at our side we can keep on walking, keep on carrying the weight of a day which only a moment before we found unbearable.

It is important to realize, of course, that Veronica cannot extinguish the pain. She can only relieve it by the power of her presence. She brings the spiritual message: Don't give up; I am with you.

ELIZABETH

Acceptance

"In my friend," Isabel Norton wrote, "I find a second self." The comment brings us up straight. How many of those are there? Not many, surely. And what does that mean for the rest of the people in our lives whom we call "friend"? The statement becomes a rubric for telling one kind of relationship from another, for making an important distinction between a "friendly" and a "friendship" relationship. Best friends, very close friends, close friends, social acquaintances, and casual acquaintance are not the same thing.

Women know the difference among relationships and treat all of them accordingly. Those who are, really, "a second self" are easily identified. These friends, our "second selves," are the ones from whom we ask no explanations, on whom we pass no judgments. They are those whose struggles and stumblings, needs and responses we know like we know our own. Others we may spend time with, we may enjoy, we may join with in common projects, but with them we do not expose our hearts in the hope of finding healing hands.

Most of all, our real friends are the ones who take us into their lives with the ease of family and the warmth of love. They have no sarcastic comments to make of us, no subtle but clear criticisms to make in our presence for our sake, no noxious remarks to make to others about us. They offer what women say they look for most in a relationship: encouragement, support, and a sense that they themselves are worthwhile human beings. Real friends are simply there for us, no matter the pressure, no matter the pain. They are home for us when no other home is open.

It's not that friends justify our failures; it is simply that they do not even notice them. Failure has nothing to do with what they see in us. Failure has nothing to do with what we do or do not disclose to them. To a real friend, whatever sins we bear are simply the lessons we've learned along the way to becoming the best in us. There is no absolution needed. Where acceptance is the idiom of the heart, everything translates into understanding. A real friend, the second self, is cut from the cloth of Elizabeth.

Elizabeth was the cousin to whom Mary of Nazareth went, betrothed, yes, but unmarried, and pregnant to someone other than Joseph "before they came together." It was a major issue, both religious and social. To be pregnant and unmarried in the Jewish community of the time was not simply to risk disapproval, it was to risk death. It was certainly to be shunned. But Elizabeth, contrary to all tradition, against all common sense, took Mary into her home, no questions asked, no verdict levied.

More than that, Elizabeth recognized in Mary the great gain that would eventually come from a situation that looked like such great loss to everyone else. Elizabeth accepted Mary for who she was, and she saw the goodness in her. Literally. Immediately.

Elizabeth's power in friendship is a fierce commitment to hold on with hope to the spiritual fecundity of a friend. However dark, however debilitating the circumstances with which the friend may be grappling at the moment, Elizabeth knows that in the end will come goodness because goodness is of the essence of the one we love as we love ourselves.

Acceptance is the ability to receive with a listening heart the friend who contravenes the social language of the time. The one who dresses differently, and talks differently, and lives differently from the norm of the neighborhood, the confines of the community. But the Elizabeths who love us take no notice of these differences. Acceptance of the differences in the other leaves room for the presence of the person and, as a result, she herself has room to become a new person.

What we accept into our lives in the other changes our own sense of what life is really about. For that reason, acceptance is never merely tolerance, it is vision. It is the new juice of soul that comes from understanding. It is what stretches my own spirit beyond the truisms of yesterday. Acceptance is its own reward.

It is the Elizabeth quality of friendship that separates the friendly from the friends, that makes a chain nothing as meaningless as the unconventional or the unorthodox can break.

Acceptance is the universal currency of real friendship. It allows the other to be the other. It puts no barriers where life should be. It does not warp or shape or wrench a person to be anything other than what they are. It simply opens its arms to hold the weary and opens its heart to hear the broken and opens its mind to see the invisible. Then, in the shelter of acceptance, a person can be free to be even something more.

RUTH

Availability

"Those who have not the weakness of friendship," Joseph Joubert wrote, "have not the strength." This observation—puzzling and profoundly disturbing as it is—stops us where we stand. We need to think a bit. We're inclined in fact to read the statement twice.

The truth is that friendship almost always comes out of our weaknesses and will demand, before it's over, the best of our strengths. That, in fact—the ability to know and admit our needs —is one of the strongest foundations of women's friendships. Women allow one another the grace of humility, and they incite, in return, a veritable outpouring of strength.

But there has been an eruption of invulnerability in Western society that threatens to swamp the truth in us, render it useless, and paralyze the process of our growth. The classic understanding of the value of humility got lost in the shuffle of the modern devotion to autonomy. Somehow or other, contemporary society came to translate humility as simpering or sycophancy or spinelessness. It lost the aura of honesty that the ages before us had ascribed to it. As a result, we have lost a sense of what is really lost when we're not honest about who we are and what we need.

Instead of humility, that raw awareness of what is lacking in us in this particular moment, in this particular situation, our age has spawned a host of workshops designed to help us "get back in touch with ourselves." There is a pathetic kind of humor in such projects.

"Getting in touch with ourselves and our feelings" is precisely an exercise which women seem to come by naturally. We no sooner discover what we lack than we are required to suppress it in order to parade as independent. As if anybody were.

But either we don't know that none of us is truly independent, or we refuse to admit it, for fear that the whole image of invincibility our society works so hard to maintain might be punctured.

Then what will happen to our reputation for effectiveness? What will happen to the whole notion that women are just as strong as men? What will happen to the icon of the totally competent, perfectly self-sufficient female? The perfect mother? The perfect wife? The perfect multitasker? The perfect professional woman?

What will happen? She will become human. She will become the kind of woman other women seek as friend, to know and understand their own weaknesses. They sense that she has navigated the shoals and storms of life before them. She is qualified to be on their side.

But friendship, the ability to companion the soul of another, is not simply situational. To become a real friendship, it must have the quality of forever. It must have a sense of "reliable alliance," of "ready availability."

There is a difference between receiving help and feeling that it is available. "It is not so much our friends' help that helps," Epicurus wrote, "as the confidence of their help." It's the liquid accessibility, the inexhaustible capital of it, that really counts. And that is why the story of Ruth, and her friendship with Naomi, gets such a grip on our hearts, on our lives.

⸺

Naomi was an old widow, sojourning in the foreign land of Moab. She had buried her husband and both her sons there. Now she had been left in her old age without the only welfare system the ancient world had to offer, the extended family. Her one hope in life, she felt, was to make the long journey back home to Bethlehem where, perhaps, some distant male relatives would have pity on her and care for her, as kinship called for. But the family ties had been long broken and chances were slim.

One of her widowed daughters-in-law, Orpah, saw Naomi on her way and then returned to Moab. But Ruth, her other Moabite daughter-in-law, also a widow, but young, pretty, and definitely remarriagable, did the unthinkable. She decided that instead of staying with her own people, her own country, she would accompany Naomi, whom she loved, into a country where she and her kind had long been considered enemy. However much Naomi attempted to dissuade her, Ruth simply refused to leave her side. "Your people will be my people," she said. "And your God will be my God." The stakes were enormous; the cost was immeasurable. Together they went.

The commitment of Ruth is the ultimate example of "ready availability."

The friend who stands by is the friend who gets us through life—at times without doing anything but being there. Yet the knowledge that a friend like Ruth is there—waiting, willing, available at any hour, under any circumstances—is what can make friendship more important than family in an age of the "Great Diaspora of Relatives."

The friendship of Ruth is the awareness that someone who does not have to care for us—no social expectations require it, no blood ties demand it—will in fact care for us to the end. Gratuitously.

All we need is the humility to admit that we require help, to acknowledge that there is a lack in us that only the love of another can resolve. As Joubert said, we must be willing to risk "the weakness of friendship."

Then, having recovered from the crisis, the sheer volume of demands, the exigencies of the present moment, we are restored, wiser than before, full of new life. Then our weakness has become our strength.

The risk, of course, is that having experienced such attention we begin to turn friendship into psychotherapy or present needs into expectation of future help. We turn a friend into a service agency. Or worse, the friend converts the gift into a debt that becomes forever unpayable.

But that is not friendship. The friend who stands by is the friend who stands by freely. The response worthy of such fidelity is my own strength, renewed and freely given now to the other. The Ruths of our world teach us not only what it means to have a friend—but also what it takes to be one.

ANNE

Nurturance

"Friends should consider themselves," Anna Letitia Barbauld said, "as the sacred guardians of each other's virtue." Friends give us something to live for when all the routine works of life have lost their savor or gone to dust. Friends give us something for which we are responsible until time takes them away or space removes them forever beyond the sounds of our voices or outside the grasps of our hands.

It is not a passive exercise, this thing we call friendship. To have a friend is to have the duty to be one. If friendship is gone about properly, seen as a position of trust, lived in the hope of fullness of soul, and practiced as both pledge and possibility, it is an enterprise of personal development that runs the risk of changing both ourselves and our friend. It says, "I will nourish your dreams and prod all the potential that is in you." I will, in other words, nourish your life as my own. "Friends," Thoreau wrote, "do not live in harmony, but melody. We do not wish for friends to feed and clothe our bodies, neighbors are kind enough for that—but to do the like office to our spirits." It is the quality of soul behind a friendship that tests its mettle and gives value to its weight. To nurture the other is to suckle their souls, to raise the sap of life in them, to bring them to ripe.

A good relationship, the soul of a friendship, rests on a number of qualities. It gives a sense of security—we know that we are not alone in life. It provides a consciousness of social belonging—we know that given this friend we now have a welcome place in the groups of which we are a part. It holds a reassurance of personal significance—we know that we are worthwhile because there is someone who thinks so when we ourselves doubt it most. It implies a promise of assistance —we know that if something happens to us, someone, somewhere will wake to the sound of the phone, and will come to help us. It opens up the prospect of guidance—we know down deep that when we are confused there is someone who will help us thread our way through the maze. And it fulfills the need for nurturance—we look for someone who will help us to become, to grow.

To know what it means to be cared for, to be treasured, to be nurtured is to know the Anne dimension of friendship.

—∞∞—

Anne, according to tradition, was the wife of Joachim and the mother of Mary of Nazareth. She is an obscure figure. Anne is known only through the apocrypha, the unofficial gospels of the early church, but real in the mind of any woman who seeks to touch the spirit of the women who are her ancestors in the long, plodding endgame of life. Anne becomes the mother of that whole long line of women who look to Mary of Nazareth, the mother of Jesus, as a model of courage and endurance, of integrity and goodness. Anne is the root that nourishes the tree. In looking to Mary as a model, we must look at Anne, as well. It was Anne who nurtured Mary to become the woman she was. It is the Annes in our own lives, that bevy of invisible women, who have nourished us as well.

The Anne quality of women's friendships is the emptying out of self that one woman does for another so that the friend may walk a smoother path than her own has been. It is the Anne quality in life when one woman teaches another how to bake bread and bathe babies and operate a computer and write proposals and apply for a position she feels she can never merit. It is the Anne quality that leads one woman to mentor another. And it is the Anne quality that reminds us of what it means to stand on the shoulders of the matri-archs who have gone before us, anonymous and invisible and uncomplaining. Because of what they gave to us unseen, we pour out ourselves on our friends. We live in the tradition of those women who prepared the way for us. Invisibly, often. Immeasurably, sometimes. Unreservedly, always. And one day, sooner or later, we ourselves all become Anne, the nurturer.

But nurturance is no small task, and it must never be confused with control or superintendency or superiority. To nurture is not to dominate. It is to enable. It is to make the person I nurture free of me. "If we would build on a sure foundation in friendship," Charlotte Brontë wrote, "we must love friends for their own sake rather than for our own."

To nurture a person is not to impose upon them a framework that, however healthy, is foreign to their soul. To nurture is to unleash the self for growth that is its own. Friendship nurtures when it provides a person the opportunity to experiment with the self and traces a watermark by which to measure the achievement. I become more of what I am by measuring myself against someone else. I do not become what I am by being directed by them. That is superintendency.

The one who nurtures me urges me on to aim for marks beyond me, holds nothing back, asks no return for the prodding but the effort of the try. The nurturer honors my self.

The model of Anne brings me to see beyond my own limited sense of self to the sight that she can see, for me, far beyond. Anne indicates the path, points the way, and then releases me to my own instincts. Anything else is control, not nurture. The nurturer begins a process for which she knows no end and which only I myself can complete.

Most of all, the nurturer does not direct; the nurturer applauds the qualities that are already in me to such a degree that I am carried along by the sound of her clapping to peak performance in the role that is my life. Because of her nurturing, I can become more than either of us ever expected. And that is the test of nurturance. "Anybody can sympathize with the sufferings of a friend," Oscar Wilde said, "but it requires a very fine nature to sympathize with a friend's success." Those who nurture well, applaud the longest.

MIRIAM

Joy

"With true friends," a Chinese proverb teaches, "even water drunk together is sweet enough." And, we could add, "champagne drunk alone is never sweet enough."

For anyone who has had to bear either the bitter or the bland without the help of friends, the truth of this insight is desperately real. In some ways, it might be easier to face the truly difficult moments of life without help than it is to face day after day of the dull ones with no one to pierce the gloom of the time, no one to color the gray days gold.

Finding someone with whom to share the water is the challenge.

There are parts of every life which, however valuable, simply have no amount of elixir in them to turn the unpalatable palatable. They grind along slowly while nothing changes and no lights glow.

Every woman experiences dullness at certain times. For too many women for far too long, however, the most unromantic demands of dailiness have been the norm. They have marked a woman's days and measured the boundaries of her horizons. They have drawn limits around possibility, and exposed the rough undercoat that underlay the sometimes gaudy colors of her "gilded cage." Everything looks good, but little or nothing feels good. Everything looks happy, but the laughs are few and far between.

Some of the things women have done for too many centuries are timeworn to the point of being insipid.

They are the tasteless parts of life that forever repeat and never end: make the beds, do the dishes, sweep the house. Often the routine is fraught with an urgency that drowns out everything else in life: rock the baby, stop the bloody nose, take care of the sicknesses of loved ones. Sometimes they come steeped in pain: bury the baby, survive the divorce, succumb to the debt.

For those times, the shape of friendship changes. Then friendship is not so much a model or a partnership. Then friendship becomes the only lifeline to joy. Then women help women celebrate.

Everybody understands the difference between a playmate and a friend. Playmates like what you like: bowling or fishing or bridge or golf. Playmates make all the games of life possible. But playmates do not change the quality of life; they simply change its routine long enough to breathe enough fresh air to make it possible to go on breathing at all.

It is one thing to seek out companions to fill the entertainment needs in life. It is another thing entirely to find the kind of companionship that makes the difficult moments in life fade into the mist of laughter or meaning. Women look for something deeper in their relationships than simply the kind of time-fillers that games can be. Women want friendships that bring new life to life's most serious moments.

Real friendship turns even the dullest parts of life into the kind of joy that makes the doing of them not simply just doable but in fact desirable. It is the quilting parties that turn long afternoons into stellar conversations. It is the walks to the park singing all the old camp songs to the children that make motherhood a glorious experience. It is nights on the porch talking in the dark about past times and new ideas and coming plans that make the hard years in between possible.

These moments are Miriam moments. In these moments we all need a Miriam in our lives.

———⊗⊗⊗———

Miriam, the sister of Moses and Aaron, walked through the desert with them, all the way from Egypt to the Promised Land. Day after dusty day, she shared with them the heat of the sun, the anxiety of the people, the uncertainty of the journey, the toils of the trip.

When the people began to complain about the sand and the food and the heat and the lack of water, Miriam was there. When Pharaoh's army appeared on the horizon, she was there. When the whole venture seemed on the edge of collapse, she was there. And when Pharaoh's army became mired in the sea—the armed Egyptians on one side of the Red Sea, the defenseless band of Hebrews on the other—she was there, too.

And that's exactly when Miriam changed the complexion of the whole long, sorry event. Scripture is clear about the respect her people had for Miriam—she was as much a leader of the women as her brothers were of the men—but scripture is equally clear about the joy she created for them in the midst of chaos and crisis: "Then the prophet Miriam, Aaron's sister, took a tambourine in her hand; and all the women went out after her with tambourines and with dancing. And Miriam sang to them: 'Sing to the LORD, for he has triumphed gloriously; horse and rider he has thrown into the sea.'"

Miriam brings to the camp in its most tenuous moment the gift of wild and unadulterated joy. More than that, she releases it in all the other women, too. She makes the rest of the trip possible. She makes the dull dailiness of trying to create a new life out of the shards of the old possible. She brings music back to the hearts of women who have known only pressure and sacrifice for weeks.

It is Miriam, the joy-giving friend in a woman's life, the friend who leads the singing when everyone else is too tired, too depressed, too discouraged to sing, who brings us all out of the dark and dull of time into the bright again.

No, all of life is not a party, and those who in their superficiality try to make it so are not our friends. They only block us from being able to see what needs to be seen in times of struggle and death, of decision making and transition. To ignore such challenges in the name of "having fun" is little more than immaturity. But, on the other hand, to have no Miriam with us to bring the kind of light to life that makes the dark way clear again is emotional deprivation of the worst kind.

"Friends are as companions on a journey," wrote

Pythagoras. "They ought to aid each other to persevere in the road to a happier life."

Miriam, the joy-maker, makes the road as she goes. If we're lucky, we know her and she takes us with her on the way.

MARY MAGDALENE

Trust and Love

Someone, somewhere wrote, "A friend is someone who knows the song in your heart and can sing it back to you when you have forgotten the words." Someone, somewhere clearly understood what real friendship is all about. My friend is the person who knows me as well as I know myself and holds that treasure, with all its soulfulness, all its struggle, in soft and tender hands.

Real friendship, then, requires two things: the transparent disclosure of the self and another's single-minded appetite to hear it and abiding commitment to treasure it. It means that I must be willing to be known and that someone, somewhere must be intent on knowing me. Then, in those long, hard times when life is shale and rain, when I forget who I am and where I'm going, this other side of me brings me home to myself again. Friendship is not mere companionship. Friendship is intimacy.

Aristotle said that there are three kinds of friends: those we cultivate for the sake of the good times they give us, those we seek out for what they can do for us, and those we love for their own sakes. "If I were pressed to say why I love him," Montaigne wrote of his deceased friend Etienne de Boetie, "I feel my only reply could be 'Because it was he, because it was I.'" Friendship, real friendship, in other words, is the blurring of two souls into one where it was thought they were separate. No price exacted. No interest paid.

Friendship is the linking of spirits. It is a spiritual act, not a social one. It is the finding of the remainder of the self. It is knowing a person before you even meet her. It might be that we not so much find a friend, but that friendship, the deathless search of the soul for itself, finds us. Then the memory of Mary Magdalene becomes clear, becomes the bellwether of the real relationship.

⸻

Mary Magdalene is the woman whom scripture calls by name in a time when women were seldom named in public documents at all. She is, in fact, named fourteen times—more than any other women in the New Testament except Mary of Nazareth, the mother of Jesus. She is clearly a very important, and apparently a very wealthy woman. Most of all, she understood who Jesus was long before anyone else did and she supported him in his wild, free-ranging, revolutionary approach to life and state and temple. She was, it seems, the leader of a group of women who "supported Jesus out of their own resources." And she never left his side for the rest of his life.

She was there at the beginning of his ministry. And she was there at the end. She was there when they were following him in cheering throngs. And she was there when they were taking his life, dashing it against the stones of temple and state, turning on him, jeering him, shouting for his death, standing by while soldiers poked and prodded him to ignominy. She tended his grave and shouted his dying glory and clung to his soul. She knew him, and she did not flinch from the knowing.

The Magdalene quality of friendship is the ability to know everything there is to know about a person, to celebrate their fortunes, to weather their straits, to chance their enemies, to accompany them in their pain and to be faithful to the end, whatever its glory, whatever its grief. The Magdalene quality is intimacy, that unshakeable immersion in the life of the other to the peak of ecstasy, to the depths of hell.

Intimacy is a dangerous thing. It comes in two flavors: pleasure and truth. The intimacy of pleasure is self-serving and exploitative. It takes from the other the most private of gifts for the sake of the self. It is the taking of the secret for the pleasure of retelling it; it is the taking of affection for the sake of satisfaction; it is the taking of the gift for the sake of being embellished; it is the taking of the other for the stature of the self.

The Magdalene quality of friendship is what distinguishes those who walk with us through the shallows of life from those who take the soundings of our soul and follow us into the depths of them. For women, intimacy is a very serious thing. The mere act of sexual exploration will never substitute for it. Nor will the simple act of self-revelation. The first may be sheer release, superficial in its bonding, short-lived in its meaning. That kind of intimacy can exist in the most destructive of relationships. The second may be nothing more than exhibitionism, the spewing forth of the self with no real concern to be heard, only the desire to be on view.

Intimacy, the Magdalene quality, is about appreciation, affection, and warmth. It is as important to the married as to the single, to the elderly woman as to the young. It is about being deeply valued, reverently respected, lovingly tended, and warmly received. It is about more than the present moment, more than the daily routine of partnership; it is about the obscure miracles and the hidden meanings of life. It is about forever. For these things, women often look to other women, to the Magdalenes of their lives, who stand by, who reach out, who watch, and who, whatever the delay, whatever the dearth of words, are content always, always to wait.

"My fellow, my companion, held most dear," Mary Sidney Herbert wrote, "my soul, my other self, my inward friend." It is, in its essence, intimacy. It is one common vision in two people so attuned, so in harmony, that whatever the uncertainty of the way, one thing is sure: This is a redeemable bond, a nexus of spirits fit for both the doubts and the iridescence of dark nights in deep woods.

EPILOGUE

It is not easy to find models of women's friendships.
By and large they were not recorded, lost like so much
else of the history of women to the dust of time,
underestimated in their own times, unnoticed throughout time, but never far from the surface, always the col-
lagen of the woman's world. What we do have, however,
is the knowledge emerging in our own day to speak of
their value, to describe their qualities. More than that,

we have models of women who embodied the best in what women value in a friend. Lydia and her love for ideas, Prisca and her sense of self, Deborah and her sustaining wisdom, Phoebe and her untiring support, Esther and her courageous leadership, Martha and her respect for truth, Veronica and her empathy, Elizabeth and her acceptance, Ruth and her unrelenting availability, Anne and her nurturance, Miriam and her abiding joy, Mary Magdalene and her undying intimacy. Out of these small shards of barely profiled lives emerge the pictures of every woman's love.

This small book is not meant to be anything more than the beginning of the cry to see the friendships between women as a strong power for good, a potential political force for the preservation of values that the world has greatly overlooked in favor of dominance and reason and individualism. But dominance has not saved us. And reason has been grossly unreasonable. Individualism made us cripplers of human community and has left us crippled ourselves, lost in a morass of solitary biases.

It is precisely in their penchant for bonding, for

tending, for befriending, for embracing, for the gathering of peoples that women's gift for the creation of human community becomes most clear. Women supported women in biblical times; women support women today. They care for one another's children, they cook one another's meals, they edit reports for one another at the office, they dry one another's tears, they applaud one another's gifts, and they build up one another's spirits through one dashed dream, one hoping generation to the next. Mothers urge daughters to be more than they were ever enabled to be. Sisters hold up sisters when everything else in life conspires to hold them down. Women carry women friends down the rutted roads of a woman's life until the friend is strong enough to make the journey on her own. Women bind themselves to other women not as prisoners are bound but as mountain climbers are linked: on loose ropes designed to save but not control.

Life for a woman is far too commonly a long and lonely climb, often difficult, customarily overlooked. The contributions of women are seldom noted. The history of women and women's place in history is seldom told. The wisdom of women is, by and large, not anthologized—is, in other words, ignored. Despite the findings of modern psychology and sociology on the nature and quality of women's friendships, for instance, even many references in this book on women's friendship come from men—because it was men's works that were printed, published, taught across time. Those days are over. Women, and the rest of the world as well, are listening for the voices of women now.

The bonding of women through contemporary groups, organizations, social circles, and public projects is now the breeding ground of a new kind of emotional life, personal development, re-creation, and even the transformation of public institutions. Women's groups expand the definition of women beyond the domestic arena to full public participation and voice.

Women's friendships and women's penchant for openness, possibility, presence, support, empathy, wisdom, truth, courage, nurturance, acceptance, joy, and intimacy are a new hope for humanity. If we can only recognize them, if we can only bring them to life—respected, revered, and invested with honor—in the world around us. For friendship is far more than a personal gift. The right friendship, rightly given, has the power to change the world. Albert Schweitzer said, "Sometimes our light goes out, but it is blown again into flame by an encounter with another human being. Each of us owes the deepest thanks to those who have rekindled the light."

What's even more important, perhaps—it lasts. Or, as Emily Brontë wrote, "Love is like the wild rose-briar; Friendship like the holly-tree. The holly is dark when the rose-briar blooms, but which will bloom most constantly?"

SCRIPTURE REFERENCES FOR
THE WOMEN IN THIS BOOK

LYDIA • *Acts of the Apostles 16:14–15*

PRISCA • *Acts of the Apostles 18:26; Letter to the Romans 16:3–4*

DEBORAH • *Judges 4:4–5:31*

PHOEBE • *Letter to the Romans 16:1–2*

ESTHER • *Book of Esther*

MARTHA OF BETHANY • *Luke 10:38–42; John 11:17–44*

VERONICA • *Luke 23:27–29*

ELIZABETH • *Luke 1:5–25, 39–45, 46–56, 57–66*

RUTH • *Book of Ruth*

ANNE • *The Infancy Gospel of James/The Protovangelion*

MIRIAM • *Exodus 14:10–15:21*

MARY MAGDALENE • *Matthew 28:1–10; Mark 16:1–11;
    John 20:11–18*